Edited by
ANDREW ROBERTS
NEIL JOHNSON
and TOM MILTON

GLADNESS AND GENEROSITY

66 They broke bread at home and ate their food **with glad and generous hearts**, praising God and having the goodwill of all the people. **99**

The Bible Reading Fellowship
15 The Chambers, Vineyard
Abingdon OX14 3FE
brf.org.uk

The Bible Reading Fellowship (BRF) is a Registered Charity (233280)

ISBN 978 0 85746 685 3
First published 2018
10 9 8 7 6 5 4 3 2 1 0
All rights reserved

Acknowledgements
Unless otherwise acknowledged, scripture quotations from The New Revised Standard
Version of the Bible, Anglicised edition, copyright © 1989, 1995 by the Division of Christian
Education of the National Council of the churches of Christ in the United States of
America. Used by permission. All rights reserved.

Scripture quotations taken from The Holy Bible, New International Version (Anglicised
edition) copyright © 1979, 1984, 2011 by Biblica. Used by permission of Hodder &
Stoughton Publishers, a Hachette UK company. All rights reserved. 'NIV' is a registered
trademark of Biblica. UK trademark number 1448790.

Photographs on pages 11, 17, 28, 32, 37, 45, 46 and 62 copyright © Tom Milton and
the Birmingham Methodist Circuit; photograph on page 4 copyright © Katie Norman;
photograph on page 52 copyright © Marty Woods.

Every effort has been made to trace and contact copyright owners for material used in
this resource. We apologise for any inadvertent omissions or errors, and would ask those
concerned to contact us so that full acknowledgement can be made in the future.

A catalogue record for this book is available from the British Library

Printed and bound by CPI Group (UK) Ltd, Croydon CR0 4YY

To order more copies of the Holy Habits resources, or to find out
how to download pages for printing or projection on screen,
please visit brfonline.org.uk/holy-habits.

Remember the context

This Holy Habit is set in the context of ten Holy Habits, and the ongoing life of your church and community.

> They devoted themselves to the apostles' teaching and fellowship, to the breaking of bread and the prayers. Awe came upon everyone, because many wonders and signs were being done by the apostles. All who believed were together and had all things in common; they would sell their possessions and goods and distribute the proceeds to all, as any had need. Day by day, as they spent much time together in the temple, they broke bread at home and ate their food **with glad and generous hearts**, praising God and having the goodwill of all the people. And day by day the Lord added to their number those who were being saved.
> ACTS 2:42–47

A prayer for the faithful practice of Holy Habits

This prayer starts with a passage from Romans 5:4–5.

> Endurance produces character, and character produces hope,
>   and hope does not disappoint us…
> Gracious and ever-loving God, we offer our lives to you.
> Help us always to be open to your Spirit in our thoughts
>   and feelings and actions.
> Support us as we seek to learn more about those habits of the Christian life
>   which, as we practise them, will form in us the character of Jesus
>   by establishing us in the way of faith, hope and love.
> Amen

The church was born in **Gladness**: **Gladness** for what God had done through the life, death and resurrection of Jesus; **Gladness** at the outpouring of the Spirit at Pentecost. There was **Gladness** in the home, in the temple and out on the streets.

In presenting his portrait of the Christian community, Luke notes in Acts that they had glad and generous hearts. The church embodied the extravagant **Generosity** that is at the heart of the divine Trinitarian community. It was a prophetic countercultural symbol in a world of avarice and greed.

Gladness and Generosity is a joyous and a challenging Holy Habit. Do enjoy its celebratory aspects and let them be a light to others. It is often in the darkest places that the light of **Gladness** or joy shines most brightly. You might like to explore **Gladness** in such settings.

As you explore the challenges represented by **Generosity**, remember that we are called to be generous with all we are and have, not just our money. Sinfulness and its consequences are marked by selfishness. Grace is expressed in **Generosity** and forgiveness. This takes us to the very heart of the gospel message. It is also a powerful challenge that comes to us from countries like South Africa and Rwanda, where people have chosen to be extraordinarily generous in forgiving. How might such testimonies inspire and change you and your church?

Gladness and Generosity is a Christian way of life. May these resources help you to walk that way ever more faithfully and fully.

 Resources particularly suitable for children and families
 Resources particularly suitable for young people

CH4   Church Hymnary 4 (also known as Hymns of Glory Songs of Praise)
RS   Rejoice and Sing
SoF   Songs of Fellowship 6
StF   Singing the Faith

Reflections

Gladness and Generosity go together in this Holy Habit because they are inextricably linked. A generously forgiving and trusting nature is often – though not necessarily – a cheerful one. The act of giving gives rise to a cheering feeling; most of us feel better after being generous to someone else. But the root of giving that is generous and cheerful is thankfulness, as we realise what God has done for us and respond with **Gladness** and joy.

There is no 'ought' about being glad – we don't choose how we feel about life – but **Gladness** is more than just a happy or cheerful feeling. Consider what it was like for New Testament churches when they heard Paul was coming – perhaps a bit like an Ofsted announcement! Yet, Paul knew the objective joy of our faith that remains whatever mood we may be in. As loving communities, we seek not just to share each other's burdens but also to share each other's joys as we respond to the **Generosity** of God.

When the then Archbishop George Carey visited Sudan in 1993, he was encouraged to meet some of the Dinka people. These proud people included many noted for their Christian faith. It was hoped the visit would show support as they faced massacres in the civil war and suffered the effects of climate change. But the Dinkas are a migrant people, and it was by no means certain that they would be found.

The visitors drove out into the scrubland to a likely place and waited to see if the Dinkas would come. They were about to give up when at last there was movement on the horizon. It was clear that the people and their herds were much depleted. They were moving slowly, looking weak and frail; the visitors were filled with sorrow and foreboding. As the Dinkas came closer, the visitors were amazed to hear them singing, and their songs were Christian songs of praise. At last they met, and together shared in the **Gladness** of worship, with the archbishop and his party feeling they were the ones who had drawn strength and blessing from the meeting.

UNDERSTANDING THE HABIT

Below are some thoughts and ideas on how you might incorporate this Holy Habit into worship. You can find more resources for worship, in which **Gladness and Generosity** is introduced, in *A Generous Life*, a special edition of *Roots* magazine, produced by the Methodist Church (**www.methodist.org.uk/mission/a-generous-life**).

Biblical material

Old Testament passages:

- Genesis 28:10–22   Jacob's dream at Bethel
- Psalms 42, 43   Longing and lament
- Psalm 100   Thanksgiving and joy
- Proverbs 11:24–35   Being blessed for **Generosity**
- Isaiah 35:1–10   A destiny of **Gladness**

Gospel passages:

- Matthew 5:1–12   **Gladness** even when persecuted
- Matthew 10:5–11   Give as freely as you have received
- Luke 1:46–55   The Magnificat
- Luke 6:27–38   The returns of **Generosity**
- Luke 10:25–37   The **Generosity** of the good Samaritan
- Luke 21:1–4   The **Generosity** of the poor
- John 12:1–8   Oil on the feet of Jesus
- John 20:19–23   Resurrection **Gladness**

Other New Testament passages:

- Acts 3:1–11   **Generosity** is not just money
- Acts 20:25–35   Supporting those in need
- 1 Corinthians 1:4–9   Giving thanks to God
- 2 Corinthians 9   God loves a cheerful giver

Suggested hymns and songs

There are a large number of hymns and songs that refer directly or indirectly to our appreciation of all that has been given to us, or offering ourselves. This selection is designed to encourage people to explore the range more.

- All people that on earth do dwell (CH4 63, RS 712, StF 1)
- Boldly I approach (The art of celebration) (SoF 2746) ☺
- Come, thou fount of every blessing (RS 360, StF 494)
- Eternal God, your love's tremendous glory (RS 33, StF 3)
- God in his love for us lent us this planet (CH4 240, RS 85, StF 727)
- God, whose farm is all creation (CH4 226, RS 612, StF 122)
- How shall I sing that majesty (CH4 128, RS 661, StF 53)
- In the wonder of creation (StF 110)
- Let all the world in every corner sing (CH4 122, RS 114, StF 57)
- Let earth and heaven agree (StF 358)
- Morning glory, starlit sky (RS 99, StF 12)
- Now thank we all our God (CH4 182, RS 72, StF 81)
- Pressed down, shaken together (Jim Bailey, SongSelect 1089012) 👪
- Shout for joy! The Lord has let us feast (CH4 676, StF 598)
- Sing of the Lord's goodness (CH4 157, StF 65)
- Sing to the Lord (SoF 2025) ☺
- Tell out my soul (CH4 286, RS 740, StF 186)
- The greatest day in history (Happy day) (SoF 2025) ☺
- This is amazing grace (SoF 3145) ☺
- This is living (SoF 3101) ☺
- We have nothing to give (StF 670)
- When all your mercies, O my God (RS 109, StF 97)
- With gladness we worship (StF 17)

Introduction to the theme 👪

You will need:

- Two boxes or baskets (shoebox size is ideal), with lids or a makeshift cover
- Twelve doughnuts (or giant cookies, cakes, pieces of fruit, etc.)
- Two plates and two knives (think safety! They don't need to be very sharp).

Place one doughnut on a plate in one of the boxes and the rest on a plate in the other. Put both boxes on a table at the front that's visible for all to see.

Open the session by explaining that, in Luke 21:1–4, we read about Jesus in the temple, watching people putting their gifts of money into the collection box. Some are wealthy and then along comes a widow, who puts just a few coins in. Jesus comments that, although she has little, what she gives is everything. She's extraordinarily generous in what she gives, despite not having much herself.

Ask how generous we feel we are (invite a show of hands – very generous, quite generous, not at all generous). Treat this as some light-hearted fun. Note that **Generosity** can be a difficult thing to do in practice.

Ask four volunteers to come and help with a task – two per box. Explain that in the box is something you'd like them to be generous with, and in a moment they can take a look and decide with each other how best to do this. Before they look, encourage them to have a quiet conversation about how they plan to be generous. While this is happening, invite people to share instances when others were generous to them – what was it like?

Ask both pairs to get ready to be generous with the contents of the boxes. Be prepared for them to respond in a variety of ways from eating the doughnuts themselves to sharing with others. Ask them why they chose to do this. Thank them for taking part.

Sum up the time by reminding everyone that being generous looks different for each of us – if both pairs gave all their doughnut(s) away for eating, highlight the fact that it doesn't matter how much we have (whether we consider it a lot or just a little), it's what we do with it that counts!

Close by showing the three-minute video, '20 Random Acts of Kindness', which you can find on YouTube (**youtu.be/AFTBBKIX760**). Challenge those gathered to list 20 random acts of kindness they could do without money and without being seen.

Thoughts for sermon preparation

Psalm 100; 1 Corinthians 1:4–9; Matthew 10:5–11

Do you remember writing thank-you letters, or equivalent, as a child? Some of us may have done that gladly, but for others of us it may be an uneasy memory, bringing back feelings of being forced to write when all that we wanted to do was play with our new toys.

At one level, forcing people to be pleased with and grateful for a present emphasises the powerlessness of the recipient and the powerfulness of the giver. Is that how God wants it to be in our relationship with him? Or is the way God deals with us more like the feelings I get when I give a child a toy, and he or she does not either ignore it or snatch and refuse to let anyone else look at it and play with it, but with a huge smile talks to me about it and generously lets me and others share in playing with it? I do not need a letter of thanks when that happens (although, of course, I might appreciate one if I was not there to have this experience).

At another level, though, we need prompting about how to respond to things. We need reminding to think of others and not be selfish. The thing about Holy Habits is that we start by learning how to look at the world with the 'mind of Christ', and how to embody that outlook in how we live. That mindset and way of living then gradually becomes habitual, until eventually they become instinctive.

Psalm 100 is one of those prompts about how to respond to things and, above all, to God. At the core of it, everything depends on what God has done, the way that God has treated us and what God is like (vv. 3, 5). That gracious **Generosity** of God lifts our spirits with joy and prompts our **Gladness** (v. 2). That **Gladness** is then channelled through thanksgiving expressed in worship and praise (vv. 2, 4).

1 Corinthians 1:4–9 shows that thanksgiving is an expression of gratitude, and gratitude is a response to grace, the love of God freely and generously given in Christ. It is important to notice that, for Paul, thanksgiving is not just a response to the grace given to Paul himself, but also for the grace he can see has been given to others. He can see that the Corinthians are being enriched in what they know of Christ, in the ways that they speak of Christ, in the testimony they give to Christ and in the gifts of the Spirit that they are developing. He sees that they are becoming more Christ-like, discerns that this is the result of God's love working in them, and thanks God for it.

The Greek words Paul uses point us towards deep spiritual and theological truths. Grace is *charis*. Thanksgiving is *eucharistia* (which is why the service of Holy Communion is often called the 'Eucharist'). When we receive the grace of God, when we recognise and accept things as gifts from God, and offer them back to him with ourselves in thanksgiving, then we receive ourselves back again from God transformed with them. The grace starts to take root in us and begins to be expressed as fruit and gifts of the Spirit, or 'charisms'. In a profound and proper sense, we become 'charismatic'.

So the love and grace of God received thankfully in worship and prayer leads to mission. Worship and mission go together inextricably. If Psalm 100 emphasises **Gladness and Generosity** being expressed through thanksgiving in worship, Matthew 10:5–11 shows them being expressed through thanksgiving in service. The key is the second half of verse 8. The generous love that the disciples have freely received from God prompts them to share it generously with others around them, not just through preaching (v. 7), but also through engaging with people practically in seeking to release them from whatever prevents them living to their full potential.

But it is also interesting to note that as the disciples receive the love of God, they are prompted not just to give gladly and generously to others, but also to receive gladly and generously from others. They are to let others give them resources and shelter (vv. 9–11). In other words, they are to be generous in letting others be generous to them.

Prayers

A collect

Most gracious God, all good things come from you and are signs of your love.
May our gratitude fill us with gladness, and our gladness with generosity,
that we may express our joy in the service of others,
and give in thankfulness for what we have received,
through Jesus Christ our Lord.
Amen

A prayer for mornings and evenings

These prayers could be used by individuals in forming this habit, or by the church as a whole. Do feel free to adapt them to fit your particular context.

In the morning…

> Joyful God, I thank you
> for this morning and for the gift of life in it,
> for this moment that you have given me to spend with you
> for the opportunity of this very day to share with you
> through the people I meet and the places I shall be…
>
> Generous God, I share with you my hopes and concerns
> for my friends and family,
> for the diversity and business of my church and my community,
> for those struggling for a living wage for all,
> for our villages, towns and cities to become places of sanctuary,
> for the work of organisations striving for the good of all…
>
> I offer all to you for transformation through your grace and love.
> Amen

In the evening…

> Joyful God, I thank you
> for one wonderful moment today.
> I live it again and savour your gift of love to me in it,
> for people I care about that I have seen or heard or thought about,
> for the challenges that haven't overwhelmed,
> and the good news that is gospel for me…
>
> Generous God, I share with you more of my hopes and concerns
> for my friends and family,
> for those who are lonely or scared tonight,
> for those who will be awake, at work or caring for loved ones,
> for those staying with all who will be born or who will die this night,
> for those who find this time of year hard…
> I offer all to you for transformation through your grace and love.
> Amen

A prayer of adoration

Creator God,

For your outpouring of generosity, for the breadth and depth of creation,
for the awesome vastness of the universe
and the invisible glory of subatomic nature, we thank you.

For the living creatures that surround us
and for the very processes of life itself, we thank you.
For our own lives as communities, families and individuals,
for the joy of working, resting and sharing together, we thank you.

For the mystery of consciousness,
for the pleasure of beauty and the exercise of understanding –
for all these things, we respond with gladness and praise.

Saviour God,

We rejoice in you as all creation rejoices to have you in our midst.
We recall John the Baptist in his mother's womb leaping for joy,
the angels singing praises and the shepherds taking up the song.
We recall the life-changing thankfulness of those you healed and blessed.
We recall the excitement of the crowds,
and the very stones eager to join your praise.

You gave your life upon the cross for all creation, the greatest gift of all,
but you were to be restored, gladness was to break forth
and tears of sorrow were exchanged for tears of joy.

Spirit God,

With the disciples, we are sometimes scared or tired,
ashamed or mystified, yet still you come.
You come to us as a sign of the love between Father and Son,
as a generous invitation to join our hearts with theirs.
The faith we profess comes alive again, the cloud parts
and the gladness of salvation blazes forth again.

May you bring to us your fruits,
and among them may you nurture in us generous spirits slow in judgement,
and generous deeds, sharing with others according to their need
and offering one another in love.

Amen

A prayer of intercession

Inspired by Luke's teaching and parables about a wedding banquet.

We pray this day for those who are rarely invited to anything:
for people who have no place to call home,
who have fallen through the cracks of society,
or been forced to leave family and work behind,
for people whose behaviour makes others fear them,
for people who simply cannot find a way in
because of the condition they carry.
Lord, help us get over our embarrassment at meeting people
who are different from ourselves.
Teach us how to be more generous hosts,
creating places of genuine welcome, accessible to all.

We pray this day for those who grab the best places
or are too busy to accept the invitation:
for all who fail to see the world that supports their privileged lifestyle,
for all who have no time to enjoy the life they have been granted,
for all who would forget their own background for fear of losing face.
Lord, help us accept and love the people you would have us be;
teach us to celebrate the gifts and successes, great and small,
that life brings to each of us.

We pray this day for all who do not feel like celebrating at all:
for people feeling the loss of someone close, or work or health,
for people who suffer from anxiety and fear or crippling shyness,
for people who are convinced that no one would want their company.
Lord, help us hold out a hand of friendship.
Teach us the words and actions that will make a difference.

We pray this day for our part in the great feast of life,
that we might know ourselves invited and tell others that they are too,
looking forward to the glorious day when your peaceable kingdom
can be celebrated by one and all together with joy.
Amen

A prayer for anxious times (based on Matthew 6:25–33)

'Do not be anxious,' you say, Jesus.
'Stop worrying about food and drink and clothing – God knows you need
 them!'
'Amen!' says my head.
But my heart says something different.

I see how God feeds the birds, clothes the lilies, provides for creation,
And yet I cannot believe God will do it for me.
I cannot trust that there will be enough food,
Enough income,
Enough pension,
Enough security.

Maybe I don't think that I am worth bothering about, that my needs matter;
Maybe it's that I cannot trust that I am loved enough;
That God notices me,
Thinks about me,
Worries for me.

Maybe I think I need to shout louder,
Try harder,
Persuade God to love me.

Maybe I fear that God treats me the way I treat others:
Taking care of myself first,
Making sure there's enough for me and mine,
Living at the expense of others
To secure my tomorrows,
Rather than trusting myself to God's open-handed generosity
And extravagant love.

Show me, Jesus,
Take me to the wilderness where five loaves feed five thousand.
Take me to the sick places, the possessed places, the hurting places
Where there is always enough time and love and grace and power to go round.
Enough – and always more – much more.
And take me to the hill
Where infinite love and forgiveness
Meet infinite sacrifice.

Confront me with your outrageous generosity,
Your wasteful, extravagant love,
Your wild freedom,
Your exuberant joy!

Unlock my heart.
Free my spirit.
Teach me to live as your child
Rather than as a beggar.
Amen

A prayer of giving thanks

This is the day, Lord,
this is the day we come to worship together.
We come because we are amazed at your generosity,
amazed at so much beauty,
so much love,
so much care offered to each and all who are open,
open to being part of your wondrous kingdom,
open to living lives of beauty and love and care.

How can we thank you for your gracious invitation?
Thank you for the joy in our lives,
for the kindness shown, even by strangers,
the moments when we have entertained angels
and not recognised them until they have left
and left us the better for their companionship.

We thank you in the everyday,
in the offered hand,
the encouraging word,
the touch of friendship.

This is the day, Lord,
each day in your presence is a day of gladness
and so we worship you, this day and always.
Amen

A prayer of adoration

Blessed are you, Lord God,
Earth-maker, star-lighter, world-lover.
You sang creation into being by the power of your word;
Yet not a sparrow falls to the ground without you knowing it,
And the very hairs on our heads are numbered!
We praise you for the mind-blowing scale of your greatness
And the searing intimacy of your love.

Blessed are you, Jesus Christ,
Truth-teller, bread-giver, kingdom-bringer.
You are Emmanuel – 'God with us';
You whispered words of love and welcome, and we howled for your crucifixion,
Yet instead of judgement, we hear your plea for us: 'Father, forgive them!'
We praise you for the shocking generosity of your grace
And the new creation you bring to birth.

Blessed are you, Holy Spirit,
Dead-raiser, joy-bringer, heart-dweller.
You are the voice of justice that inspired the prophets
and the power that raised Jesus from the dead,
Yet you make us your dwelling place, intimately,
filling us with the very life of God.
We praise you for the abundant life that you bring
And your presence with us, moment by moment.

Glory to you, God our Father!
Glory to you, God our Brother!
Glory to you, God our Life!
Amen

A prayer of confession

Generous God, we don't 'do' abundance.
We see scarcity all around us.
The threat of our own lack preoccupies us.
We clutch and grab for ourselves.
We do not trust in your provision for tomorrow.

We opt for survival when you offer us abundant life.
We hanker for the safety of yesterday,
when you call us into the glorious adventure of tomorrow.
We shrink from generosity and call it 'stewardship'.
We live in paralysing fear when you offer us extravagant love.

Blow open our minds,
Blow open our hearts,
Blow open our spirits,
Blow open our wallets

Until we are overwhelmed by your extravagance,
Transformed by your generosity
And liberated by your abundance
To be the answer to the prayers of others.
Amen

A liturgy for a Love Feast

This liturgy was composed by Jill Barber (a former Vice President of the Methodist Conference) and includes some material from the Northumbria Community used with permission (confession from 'A Celtic Communion' in *Celtic Daily Prayer Book 2*, 2015; excerpt from the Oswald liturgy in *Celtic Daily Prayer Book 1*, 2015). The material is readily available in other hymn/song books. Alternatively, other appropriate songs could be used.

Prayers of praise
(After each line, people call out adjectives, phrases or names that ascribe honour and praise.)

We praise God the Father, for God is…
We praise God the Son, for Jesus is…
We praise God the Spirit, for she is…

Holy God, three in one, we praise your holy name. Amen

Prayers of confession and assurance
We are here, God, in this moment, in this place, and we thank you that you are here with us. You know us, God, we do not have to pretend with you.

In the silence of your love, we bring you the things that trouble us, that harm us, that make us feel ashamed or afraid.

(*Silence*)

We share those things that are common to us, as citizens of this country… or members of the same church or local community…

(*Silence*)

Listen to the words of Jesus, words that we can trust:
'Do not be afraid, your sins are forgiven. Come and follow me.'
Thanks be to God.
Amen

Brother, sister, let me serve you (StF 611)

Prayer of openness
We come to God, aware that we need God with every fibre of our being. We want nothing to stand between us. We draw near, and as we are held, we slowly dare to look into the face of the One who holds us… and gradually our own faces and our lives begin to reflect his beauty.

Read John 20:19–23. Imagine yourself as one who was there. What emotions do you experience? How does it change you… or not? What brings us peace when we are troubled?

Lord, this day is your gift to me […]
I thank you for the wonder of it.

All that I am, Lord, **I place into your hands.**

All that I do, Lord, **I place into your hands.**

Everything I work for, **I place into your hands.**

Everything I hope for, **I place into your hands.**

The troubles that weary me, **I place into your hands.**

The thoughts that disturb me… **I place into your hands.**

Each that I pray for… **I place into your hands.**

Each that I care for… **I place into your hands.**

Treasures from our journey
(*In groups, share something of the story of those people who have inspired you, or been significant to you on your faith journey.*)

Glory to God (StF 753)

Love Feast blessing
Be present at our table, Lord;
be here and everywhere adored;
thy creatures bless, and grant that we
may feast in paradise with thee.   [*John Cennick, 1741*]

Sharing of the cake
(*The cake is passed around the group. Each person takes a piece, and shares something for which they are thankful to God.*)

Sung response (Taizé song): **In the Lord, I'll be ever thankful** (StF 776)

Passing of the loving cup
(*A jug of water is passed around the group, and each person's cup is filled in turn. When your cup is filled, hold it and give thanks for the person who filled it for you. Then drink, and then fill your neighbour's cup.*)

Different ways of praying

Bitter sweet – a personal prayer

Give everyone a chocolate lime sweet.

As people taste the lime, invite them to offer the bitter things in life to God. Remind them that it's okay to bring our dissatisfaction and sorrows to God.

As they taste the sweetness of the chocolate, invite them to give thanks for the good things in life. Remind them that just as the flavour of chocolate transforms the taste of the lime, so God can transform our lives and bring good out of the difficult times.

Prayers of thanksgiving

Ask the congregation to share their news and keep a note of what they have said.

Explain that prayers can be said loudly as well as quietly. To the words 'God is good', invite the congregation to respond, 'Hallelujah'. Tell them that the response will sometimes be loud and sometimes quiet.

Turn each piece of news into a prayer and vary the volume of your bidding to match the prayer. The congregation should take their lead from you.

Build each response louder or softer as seems appropriate.

Creative movement and dance

Dance and creative movement can be used to express any of the Holy Habits, but is perhaps particularly appropriate in expressing **Gladness and Generosity**. For more on the use of creative movement and dance in worship, see the 'Going further with the habit' section of this booklet (p. 49).

GROUP MAT

Some of these small group materials are traditional Bible studies, some are more diverse session plans and others are short activities, reflections and discussions. Please choose materials appropriate to whatever group you are working with.

Gladness

Psalms 42, 43, 100

The psalms are a wonderful collection of poems and songs that soar the heights and plumb the depths of human experience, offering all to God in both praise and lament. In this session, we will look at three contrasting psalms.

The first is Psalm 100, from which Leona von Brethorst wrote the worship song 'I will enter his gates with thanksgiving in my heart'. The psalm:

- is a psalm of celebration which was used as a hymn in public worship and by families and individuals at home
- expresses confidence in God and specifically the goodness of God
- conveys a powerful sense of God caring for 'his people'
- encourages **Gladness** in **Worship** and **Serving** (the first verb in verse 2 can be translated as worship or serve).

Spend some time in conversation around the following questions or questions that arise in your group about the psalm.

- When and where might it be appropriate to use this psalm? (Note the point about worship and service above.)
- How might it be appropriate to use this psalm (e.g. as a poem, or a song, or via visual art, or in some form on social media)?
- For whom might this psalm be difficult at this time?

Following your consideration of the last question, move on to read Psalms 42 and 43 (which commentators suggest were originally one psalm). These are psalms of longing and lament that contrast with the joy and celebration of Psalm 100. Psalm

42 has also inspired a song, 'As the deer pants for the water' by Martin Nystrom. Notice how Nystrom takes the first two despairing lines of the psalm and then follows these with an expression of very positive worship. Is this helpful or not?

Psalms 42 and 43:

- are believed to express the cries of an individual; possibly someone in exile or suffering from illness which cut them off from the worshipping community
- are very honest accounts of despair
- express a deep thirst-like longing for God from a place of difficulty
- have a repeated refrain in which despair and hope wrestle with each other (42:5, 11 and 43:5)
- remember days of **Gladness** in the past (42:4) and look forward to days of joy in the future (43:4).

Spend some time in conversation. Please note that this could lead to deep and personal conversation, so handle it with care and confidentiality.

- Are there times when we feel like the psalmist, more inclined to despair than worship?
- How could these psalms help us to express our doubts, our despairing thoughts, our tears?
- How might the references to hope in the psalms help us to find a peaceful and assuring **Gladness** in times of difficulty? Can anyone think of someone they know who has shown such **Gladness** in what otherwise would be a place of complete despair? (If you need an example of such a person, please see the story of Joy on p. 50.)

Activity

Invite people to create a card or a picture based on the words and images of these psalms to give to someone or to keep for themselves. Provide people with art and craft materials to do this. (The artwork of Hannah Dunnett or Mary Fleeson could provide helpful examples if needed.)

Alternatively, people could take photographs to capture the essence of any of the psalms or have a go at writing their own psalm to express how they feel at this time.

You might like to conclude the session by reading the psalms again, or singing the songs based upon them, before offering all the thoughts and feelings that have emerged in the session to God in prayer.

Generosity

Genesis 28:10–22

The idea of **Generosity** can be applied to various aspects of our lives. Most commonly, it is used in connection with giving away money – so we will start there.

Be warned: discussion on anything to do with money can prove very sensitive. A famous evangelist said that the last part of a person to be converted is their wallet. But the Bible frequently talks about money, so if you are serious about developing Holy Habits, don't skip this.

What is generosity?

To say someone is generous implies they give away more than would normally be expected in the circumstances. But what is normal? What line has to be crossed before we are deemed generous? How can being truly generous become a habit?

Read Genesis 28:10–22.

Here is one starting point for biblical hints about **Generosity**. Notice that:

1 Jacob is not at this point full of **Gladness**, secure and happy, but is lonely, vulnerable and unsure of his future.
2 God does not make Jacob rich, but assures him of God's care for him.
3 Jacob decides that if that promise proves true, he will respond gratefully by giving ten per cent of his resources back to God.

This idea of giving a tenth to God – a tithe – occurs in several places in the Old Testament. It is the first tenth, with the implication that you live on whatever is left; this sort of **Generosity** is not based on what cash you have left over after you have paid all your bills.

Christians would see in Jesus even more profound reasons to be grateful to God than Jacob could imagine.

- If giving is a response to a God whose love is infinite, can any amount be deemed adequate, let alone generous?
- Is **Generosity** any more than just giving a bit more than the people around us?

A habit of generosity

Some Christians see tithing as the Christian standard for **Generosity**. They may teach their children as soon as they have pocket money to put some of it in the church collection to start a habit of giving. John Wesley, when a young man, calculated how much he needed to live on, and for the rest of his life spent only that amount on himself; whatever other income he acquired, he was free to give away.

- What experiences in your life shape what you think of as **Generosity** today?
- Has your **Generosity** been most helped by a regular pattern or by spontaneous responses to needs?

Debating the tithe

Jacob did not live in 21st-century Britain. Some Christians argue that a ten per cent benchmark for giving is inappropriate now when government, through the welfare state, provides many of the social support structures that the tithes might have covered in Jacob's day.

- Make a list of twelve things you regularly spend money on that would surprise Jacob. If you are much richer than him, is a ten per cent threshold really too high or actually too low to count as **Generosity** today?
- Do you pay your taxes in a spirit of **Generosity** towards those who benefit from public services?

Another objection to using the tithe as a modern benchmark is that giving can only be deemed generous if it is freely chosen and not just in response to a rule.

- Is it possible to develop Holy Habits without holy guidelines?
- Does giving only become truly generous if it exceeds the usual guidelines?
- For a Christian, is giving to charity morally equivalent to 'giving to God'?

The tithe can help focus a discussion on **Generosity**, but is dangerous if it excuses us from thinking about how we use the money we keep back for our own use, whether 90% or any other proportion.

- What would **Generosity** look like in the light of the choices we make for the money we spend on ourselves?
- Is spending on other family members an obligation or **Generosity** or both?

Not just money
How about working through this study again, but now relating the idea of the tithe to the ways you use your time?

The good Samaritan ☺

Luke 10:25–37

This needs to happen in a comfortable space but one where there is room for acting. The group can be any size, but up to ten people will probably be best.

Ask all the participants to say their names and give an example of someone being mean to them and how they felt. You could give it to them as a sentence to fill in: 'Someone was mean to me by _____ and I felt _____.' Then ask them to give an example of someone being generous to them and how it felt.

Read the parable of the good Samaritan (Luke 10:25–37). Use whichever translation you prefer. Ask someone who is confident reading or read it yourself. As the passage is being read, ask the group to think about who was mean in the story and who was generous.

This can then lead into a discussion about why certain people appeared to be mean and in what ways the 'good Samaritan' was generous.

If the group is slow to respond, encourage them by making the following points: the good Samaritan risked himself – were the robbers still about? He crossed cultural lines. He gave of his time and energy. He gave of his money. Did he expect a reward? The injured man was in pain, felt abandoned and then unsure of the stranger, but then thankful and glad.

This can lead into some drama in today's context. How much guidance people need will depend upon your knowledge of them. You might find the following suggestions helpful:

- Work in groups of four or five – which may of course mean doubling-up of roles.
- Encourage people to think of a scenario that brings out meanness, generosity and gladness. If they are struggling, discuss this as a whole group, giving examples before they prepare their drama. The drama could be a modern-day version of the good Samaritan, but it doesn't have to be. It could be a completely different story which brings out the themes of meanness, generosity and gladness.
- Suggested scenarios could be:
  - examples from the meanness and generosity which they shared at the beginning
  - difficulties that migrants face when they arrive in a new country
  - out shopping buying presents and seeing someone homeless in the doorway.

When the dramas have been performed, have a final discussion. It is unlikely that you will have time to think about all the points that are raised, but there might be enough for a follow-up session. Use the promptings from earlier – who was mean and who was generous? Can we always be generous, or do we sometimes have to be mean?

Then go around the group and ask them to share a way they think they will be generous during the next week and why.

Finally, share in a prayer together (you could use one from the 'Prayers' section of this booklet, starting on p. 14).

Spending money discussion 👪 ☺

Print out some paper money, all in different amounts (e.g. £10, £50 notes). Print out some pictures of (or to represent) things like a games console, smartphone, savings, charity logo, gifts to parents, holiday away, etc. and distribute them around the room.

Give each person £500 to spend and ask them to go around the room placing their money on what they would like to spend it on.

Then have a discussion about what everyone did and why. Were they generous to others?

Cake giveaway 👪 ☺

Spend one of your sessions baking cakes together and then give them away!

Reflect with the group afterwards how it felt to be generous with the cakes and what responses they received. In the giving and receiving, what **Gladness** was there?

Going without 👪 ☺

Challenge the group to give up something that they love for a fortnight or a month, for example playing with a favourite toy or using a social media account.

Afterwards, discuss what it felt like – has it made them more grateful for what they have? Has it made them more or less likely to be generous with what they have in the future? Has the experience helped them to be appreciative of other things?

Consider whether you could give up this thing on a regular basis. In what ways could you 'waste this time' with God instead?

Thankfulness reflection 👪 ☺

As a group, make a list of all the things that you have to be thankful for. These don't all have to be expensive gadgets, but could be having clean water, access to education, your own bedroom, the ability to walk, a computer, bike, etc.

You could make a 'Count your blessings' collage, or just write it on flipchart paper.

Spend some time individually reflecting on what you have and offering thanks to God. You may choose to play some quiet music while the group does this.

Invite people to set themselves a personal challenge by writing down three ways that they can be more appreciative of, or generous with, what they have. You may like to revisit this in a future session to see if they have met their challenge.

Homelessness discussion ☺

Have a session exploring the issues of homelessness or poverty. Could you invite someone in from a local charity to speak to the group about these issues?

Explore the causes of homelessness and what could be done about it. What sort of **Generosity** is needed in this context? How does this issue inform our understanding of **Gladness**?

Encourage your group to give up something that they spend money on (e.g. sweets) and give the money instead to a charity that works to tackle poverty. Spend some time praying about these issues.

Generosity storytelling 👪 ☺

Gather some real-life stories of people who have shown **Generosity** in different ways and share these with the group.

Discuss how it feels hearing the stories.

Over the following weeks, encourage the group to share their own stories of where they have been generous or witnessed **Generosity** in others.

FORMING THE HABIT

The ideas presented in this section are offered to help you establish or further practise **Gladness and Generosity** as a regular habit personally, as a church and in engagement with your local community and the wider world. You may want to consider using the ideas in more than one of these contexts.

In developing **Gladness and Generosity** as a regular habit, you may find some of the material in the 'Understanding the habit' section helpful too.

STORIES TO SHOW THE HABIT FORMING

How could you use these formative and transformative stories to inspire others? What stories of your own could you share?

In an age when many are anxious about the future, **Gladness** can change the landscape:

> In a prescient piece, Richard Vautrey, GP and former Vice President of the Methodist Conference, suggests that any church concerned that they may be dying should adopt the kind of attitude wonderfully demonstrated by the inspirational cancer patient Stephen Sutton (**www.facebook.com/ StephensStory**), having fun while living life to the max with whatever time is left, giving away as much as possible. There is a glorious, godly irony in this: for any church that is marked by generosity and knows how to party as well as how to pray, may well not die at all.
>
> 'Patients who know they are going to die often have a very different outlook on life. They make the most of every precious day. Yes, they prepare and put their affairs in order, but many also compile bucket lists of exciting and challenging things to do while they have the strength and energy to do them. They do things they never thought themselves capable of.
>
> 'So let's not dwell on our pain but instead celebrate each God-given day we have left. Let's not worry too much about long detailed plans and being too "methodical", let's instead experiment, take risks and have fun while we do so. Let's share our joy for life with those around us and let's spend the inheritance saved up by the saints who have gone before us, not with a sense of gloom as we mourn our own loss, but with joy and gratitude for the generosity of an ever-present God.'
>
> *Methodist Recorder*, 20 June 2014

Offering true forgiveness is one of the most generous acts possible. In Rwanda, nearly a million people were massacred in three months of 1994, many previously close friends and neighbours. Since then, extraordinary stories have emerged of generosity being exercised by way of forgiveness and reconciliation. Immaculée Ilibagiza tells of the day she came face-to-face with Felicien, a man she had known from childhood and with whose children she had played – a man who went on to murder her mother (Rose) and her brother (Damescene) in the Rwandan genocide.

His dirty clothing hung from his emaciated frame in tatters. His skin was sallow, bruised and broken; and his eyes were filmed and crusted. His once handsome face was hidden beneath a filthy, matted beard; and his bare feet were covered in open, running sores.

I wept at the sight of his suffering. Felicien had let the devil enter his heart, and the evil had ruined his life like a cancer in his soul. He was now the victim of his victims, destined to live in torment and regret. I was overwhelmed with pity for the man.

'He looted your parents' home and robbed your family's plantation, Immaculée. We found your Dad's farm machinery at his house, didn't we?' Semana yelled at Felicien. 'After he killed Rose and Damescene, he kept looking for you… he wanted you dead so he could take over your property.'

I flinched, letting out an involuntary gasp. Semana looked at me, stunned by my reaction and confused by the tears streaming down my face. He grabbed Felicien by the shirt collar and hauled him to his feet. 'What do you have to say to Immaculée?'

Felicien was sobbing. I could feel his shame. He looked up at me for only a moment, but our eyes met. I reached out, touched his hands lightly, and quietly said what I'd come to say.

'I forgive you.'
Immaculée Ilibagiza, *Left to Tell* (Hay House, 2007), p. 263

How does this story affect your attitude towards **Gladness and Generosity**?

The story of Love Stourbridge, in the West Midlands, shows churches coming together in **Gladness** to show **Generosity** to their community:

> Imagine if people started doing generous things for others, like acts of random kindness. Over the last few years, churches in Stourbridge, West Midlands, have been demonstrating God's unconditional love through the 'Love Stourbridge' initiative. Here are a few examples:
>
> - We run a free fun day in the local park with a high-quality live music stage, face-painting, craft activities, climbing wall, 'Say One For Me' prayer tent, graffiti wall, fair trade, kite making and debt advice.
> - We gave a free rose to 1,000 people as a 'Random Act of Kindness'.
> - We gave a free bottle of water to 600+ commuters.
> - We worked with the local retail mall to provide shoppers with free face-painting, nail art, hair-braiding, shoe-shining and live music.
> - We ran a children's holiday club attended by 100+ local children each day.
> - Our young people worked to clear overgrown gardens and remove rubbish.
> - We hosted an afternoon tea for older people, with live music and food.
> - Street Pastors gave out free packets of dates to Muslim taxi drivers for them to use at the end of each day of fasting during the month of Ramadan.
> - We baked cakes for the local uniformed services (police, fire and ambulance).
>
> Jesus said, 'Let your light shine before others, that they may see your good deeds and glorify your Father in heaven' (Matthew 5:16, NIV). To mobilise our church attenders and to stimulate their imagination, we provide them with an A to Z of Random Acts of Kindness. To maximise impact, we want their acts to be quirky, quality, substantive and socially responsible.
>
> But how can recipients glorify their Father in heaven if they don't know what's behind the Random Act of Kindness? Consequently, we encourage people to give or attach a Love Stourbridge business card to explain what they've received and why, and to encourage them to 'pay it forward'. 'Do to others as you would have them do to you' (Luke 6:31).
>
> Love Stourbridge has helped us build a positive working relationship with retailers and our local Council, and has increased the visibility and credibility of the church in Stourbridge.

You can find out more about Love Stourbridge in their promotional video: **www.vimeo.com/176928080.**

Lea Road URC, in Wolverhampton, has a long history of engaging with its neighbours. Their minister, Revd Dr Sue Walker, explains:

Ventures over the years have included a large open youth club, a day centre for elderly people and a community café. In 2012, the church was approached by the Traveller Education Service who proposed working with us to set up a project to serve the needs of people from the Roma (Gypsy) community who were arriving in Wolverhampton from various parts of Eastern Europe.

Roma people are designated as a marginalised and hard-to-reach community. The fact that Roma people were moving into the locality, an area of considerable deprivation, in which many residents face serious and complex issues related to migration and poverty, meant the church could envisage the potential for problems of various sorts. Consequently, Lea Road decided to respond positively to the opportunity to open their doors in welcome to their new neighbours.

Through meetings with a few members of the Roma community, trust was built and an understanding of their culture and awareness of their needs led to a weekly drop-in session being started on the church premises. Activities on offer at the drop-in include:

- a place of welcome and refreshment in the church community café
- opportunities to meet local people, including church members
- opportunities for project attendees to cook meals and express their culture
- help with form-filling; informal support with English language
- opportunities to listen to talks from relevant professionals
- opportunities to attend self-esteem building workshops
- arts, crafts and sports activities for the children
- occasional social events.

Through people working together, this project has successfully broken down barriers within the local community and has built bridges. This has led to people from the Roma community gaining a better understanding of British life and culture and a greater understanding of support mechanisms available to them. In turn, the church and community now have a better understanding of Roma culture and everyone has some new friends.

We do not know what the future holds, but are trusting that God will continue to lead us to find new ways of sharing the love of Jesus unconditionally with our neighbours and, in turn, receiving from them too.

PRACTICES

Here are some suggestions for how **Gladness and Generosity** can be part of a rhythm or rule of life in our personal discipleship and in and through the fellowship of our churches.

When we experience the generous, extravagant love and grace of God, a natural response is to pass on that **Generosity** to others. Churches are often places where people are found to be generous with their gifts and their time, with activities organised for church and community members of all ages. As you embrace this habit, make time to take stock of what you are already doing as individuals and as a church to pass on that **Generosity** and expression of God's love to others. You may already be at full capacity, or there may be ideas suggested elsewhere in the booklet that you might like to adopt. Are you doing something that you once offered in **Gladness and Generosity**, but that has now become a chore? Is it still fulfilling its original purpose or has the need changed?

But could the 'doing' part be the easy bit? The biggest challenge of this habit is not **Generosity**, but **Gladness**. Churches are often full of busy people doing all sorts of good things for very good reasons. Do we always practise **Generosity** with **Gladness**? If we are so busy doing good that we are too tired to be kind (and glad) to those around us, does that diminish the generous act? Our attitude, our very being, is so much more important, for this is what really speaks to those around us. In Acts 2, the passage from which the idea of Holy Habits was conceived, we are told that 'day by day the Lord added to their number those who were being saved'. How much of this was to do with the fact that the people were acting 'with glad and generous hearts'?

2 Corinthians 9:7 says, 'Each of you must give as you have made up your mind, not reluctantly or under compulsion, for God loves a cheerful giver.' So, as you learn about the Holy Habit of **Gladness and Generosity** and as you seek to make this a habit that really sticks, by all means be generous with your time and your talents, but not at the expense of being generous with your attitude. There may be some things you need to give up in order to be able to practise **Generosity** with **Gladness**. What do you need to do and how do you need to 'be' to ensure that **Gladness** *and* **Generosity** become part of who you are, both as individuals and as a church?

Often (daily or weekly)

Journalling

Journalling is regularly reflecting on your experiences, thoughts and encounters with God and keeping a note of your reflections. See the Holy Habits Introductory Guide for more information.

As you try different ways to develop the habit of **Gladness and Generosity** in your day-to-day life, note in your journal what you did and how you felt, and anything that was a positive experience. What have you been most thankful for? When do you find it easy or difficult to be generous? Why do you think that is? How has God challenged you? Have you noticed **Gladness and Generosity** becoming more of a habit?

What am I glad for today?

Note down what you have been most glad about today. You could write this into your journal and get into the habit of doing that every day. Or you could have a list which is kept somewhere visible that you add to throughout the day – for example, put the list on a kitchen cupboard door or the fridge door. Everyone in the household could add to the list.

As well as doing this as an individual, try it as a church. Start every church meeting with what the church has to be glad about that day or week.

Random acts of kindness

Try to do a small act of kindness for someone else every day or once a week.

Many people who do random acts of kindness keep it anonymous and often it is for a stranger. There are many ways you can show kindness; it just takes a little thought, and it doesn't have to be time-consuming or expensive.

You could do this individually or as a group (e.g. a house group or youth group). You could write about your acts of kindness in your journal.

Take a look at the Random Acts of Kindness website for more ideas: **www. randomactsofkindness.org/kindness-ideas**.

Be generous with your money

When thinking about **Generosity**, we cannot ignore the subject of financial and material **Generosity**. Everything belongs to God. Taking this into consideration changes the way we think about money, about possessions and about what we do with them. Good stewardship of resources is a biblical imperative. Remembering that all we have belongs to God might make us consider how often we give people a lift in 'our cars', how generous we are with who stays in 'our houses' or how often we invite people to share 'our food' at 'our table' at home. We might want to think about how we open up 'our church premises' or consider inviting user groups or members of the community to share (free) food with us. What a radical (and challenging) change in mindset to the way society usually works, to think of everything as God's, not ours!

But it will only be radical if it becomes more than a one-off assessment of our finances and possessions, and changes the way we live; if it becomes a Holy Habit that is part of who we are, influencing every decision we make about our possessions and finances. This challenge then must apply to 'our money' – how we spend it, how we save it, how we invest it and how we give it away. It must apply to our personal finances and those of our church. If it is to become a habit, it must always be on the agenda and influence every decision about our property and finances.

As individuals and as a church, take time to sit down and pray about your possessions and finances. They are God's good gifts to you. How can you use them for God's glory? Are there people you could be generous towards with them? Think about your giving to your church (not just what you give, but how you give). Or, together with others, think about how your church is generous to its community. Make sure this is not something you do just once as you are forming the habit. If it's to become a habit, then it needs to be reviewed regularly, every time you consider finances and possessions.

Sometimes (weekly or monthly)

Have a party ☺

The team at Lozells Methodist Church, Birmingham have been working through a Holy Habits programme. They share their party habit:

Is having a party a Holy Habit? Well it's not one of the ten, but it's certainly a great way of exploring and living **Gladness and Generosity** and many of the other Holy Habits too!

Eating Together was the first Holy Habit we explored. We invited our small, diverse congregation, from nine different countries, to bring families and friends and food to share two hours of fun and delicious food. We didn't call it a party, but when we started exploring our next Holy Habit, **Making More Disciples**, the first question was: when are we having the party? This continued throughout **Gladness and Generosity** and then there was **Breaking Bread**, with a bread maker in the corner – filling the room with bread aroma, providing bread for worship the next day. Each party the same – but different as we discover a new Holy Habit together. We plan to continue partying as we explore **Prayer**, **Biblical Teaching**, **Sharing Resources** and **Giving**.

We are learning about all ten Holy Habits with excitement and our 'Party Habit' helps us celebrate them all at once! By taking time from our busy schedule to practise the Holy Habits through partying, we have **Fellowship** together and extend our love and warmth, **Serving** families and friends outside of the church. Food and drinks bring all God's children together from different nationalities.

Be generous with what your church has

There are some stunning stories of the generous release of church buildings by faithful but dwindling congregations, that have led to the birth of fresh expressions of church that have seen many people, including many younger people, become disciples. Great examples include Tubestation in Polzeath, Cornwall (**community. sharetheguide.org/stories/tubestation**) and The Wesley Playhouse in Howden Clough, West Yorkshire (**community.sharetheguide.org/stories/playhouse**).

And of course, you don't have to be dwindling to be generous! Many thriving churches are generous with their buildings, their volunteering and their money – see for instance the story of the Roma drop-in at Lea Road URC, Wolverhampton (p. 39).

Give of yourself – literally

Fleshandblood is a campaign to encourage the church to see blood and organ donation as part of its giving. The campaign asks you to make three commitments and helps to resource you to keep them.

1 **Donate together**
    Make registering to become a blood or organ donor part of your giving and regularly encourage and help to organise visits to local blood donor sessions.

2 **Talk about donation**
    Integrate donation into areas of your teaching, help your congregation discuss donation and give opportunities to share stories.

3 **Raise awareness in your community**
    Provide information, host an event, connect with local schools, or join in during blood week and transplant week.

Find out more on the Fleshandblood website (**www.fleshandblood.org**).

City of Sanctuary and Places of Welcome

Could your church express **Generosity** to those seeking safety and sanctuary by being part of the City of Sanctuary (**www.cityofsanctuary.org**) or Places of Welcome (**www.placesofwelcome.org**) movements? These UK-wide movements are committed to building a culture of hospitality and welcome, particularly for refugees seeking relief from war and persecution. Their networks of local groups include boroughs, towns, cities, churches and other locations. Their commitment is to help refugees in particular feel safe, and to find others who will welcome them.

If going through the formal process of forming a town or city of sanctuary or place of welcome might take some time, why not seek to apply the principles behind them to the life of your church in the meantime?

Give!

Sometimes **Gladness and Generosity** are experienced in **Serving** others.

Perhaps you could share the habit of **Gladness and Generosity** with your friends and neighbours. How about inviting someone around for a cuppa or a meal? Is there someone nearby who would welcome help with their garden, the shopping, the school run, babysitting or a lift to an appointment? How could this become a habit (not necessarily doing the same thing but practising **Gladness and Generosity**)?

What could you as a church do to spread **Gladness and Generosity** between your small groups, your user groups, in your community or in your local Churches Together or interfaith group? Could you do a litter pick of the neighbourhood, plant some flowers or bulbs in a piece of wasteland, offer a cuppa to passing commuters or parents on return from the school run or choose an idea specific to the season? How will you ensure that this becomes a habit (again, not necessarily doing the same thing but consciously practising **Gladness and Generosity**)?

Occasionally (quarterly, annually)

Have a generosity audit

Conduct a 'generosity audit'. How do you use what God has given you? Review all that you have: your resources, time, gifts and experiences. This could be done as an individual, a family, a congregation or in any other group you are part of.

At different stages of our lives, the balance of giving and receiving may change. Giving should not be a burden, but a means of blessing for both giver and receiver.

Seasonal opportunities

Times in the Christian calendar offer good opportunities to practise **Gladness and Generosity**. Could any of these be used in your church annual routines?

How about holding a 'Secret Santa' among your local group of churches? Could you offer a Christmas gift to places of worship of other faiths?

Take the Love Life/Live Lent challenge which invites participants to a different action each day in Lent (**www.chpublishing.co.uk/features/love-life-live-lent**). Or if you want to 'Do Lent generously', try 40Acts (**www.40acts.org.uk**).

Maybe at Easter, you could give Easter eggs to members of the groups that meet on your premises or deliver them to local homes. Think about how your church engages with Christian Aid week. As well as collecting money or holding special services, are there ways in which you could share something of the work of Christian Aid with those who live in your community?

If you already collect gifts of food for a local charity such as a food bank at harvest, is there any way in which that could become a habit, either by collecting through the year or perhaps by gifting your time as a volunteer?

These questions will help your church to consider how it can review the place of **Gladness and Generosity** in all of its life together. They are intended to be asked regularly rather than considered once and then forgotten. You will need to determine where in your church the responsibility for each question lies – with the whole church in a general meeting, or with the church leadership, a relevant committee or another grouping. Feel free to add more of your own.

Generosity

- How generous is your welcome of visitors and newcomers? In what practical ways is this expressed?
- How generous is your church budget to partner churches, the local community, the wider world? How much of your budget is given away to bless others?
- What is your church's attitude to its property and possessions? How generously do you share your premises?

- How generous towards God and others are your worship and prayers?
- How generously do you open up opportunities for others to lead, serve and form policy?
- How generously do you let go in order to let others, particularly younger people, have a go?
- How generous are you in your discussions, conversations and meetings? What things does your church do that are ungenerous?
- How is your church generous with its words and its forgiveness?

Gladness

- What would it mean for your church to express **Gladness**? What in your church are you glad about?
- What stops you from feeling glad? What are the obstacles? What can you do to overcome them?
- Do you sometimes put on events with

the congregation or the community just to be generous or glad?
- Do members of your congregation or community think of celebrating in church on such occasions as special wedding anniversaries or 'big' birthdays?

CONNECTING THE HABITS

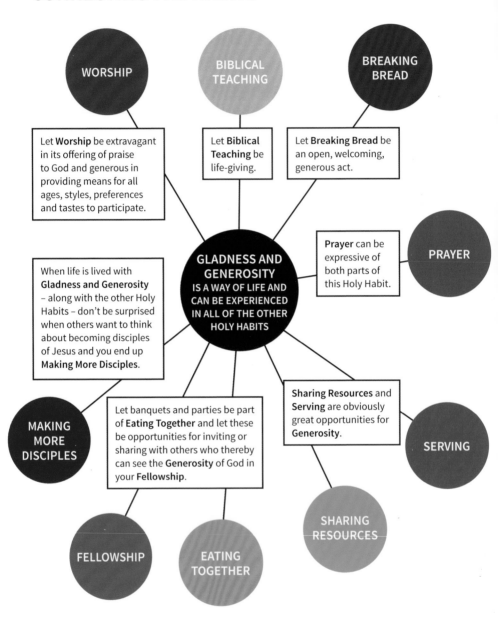

WORSHIP

BIBLICAL TEACHING

BREAKING BREAD

Let **Worship** be extravagant in its offering of praise to God and generous in providing means for all ages, styles, preferences and tastes to participate.

Let **Biblical Teaching** be life-giving.

Let **Breaking Bread** be an open, welcoming, generous act.

PRAYER

Prayer can be expressive of both parts of this Holy Habit.

GLADNESS AND GENEROSITY IS A WAY OF LIFE AND CAN BE EXPERIENCED IN ALL OF THE OTHER HOLY HABITS

When life is lived with **Gladness and Generosity** – along with the other Holy Habits – don't be surprised when others want to think about becoming disciples of Jesus and you end up **Making More Disciples**.

MAKING MORE DISCIPLES

Let banquets and parties be part of **Eating Together** and let these be opportunities for inviting or sharing with others who thereby can see the **Generosity** of God in your **Fellowship**.

Sharing Resources and **Serving** are obviously great opportunities for **Generosity**.

SERVING

SHARING RESOURCES

FELLOWSHIP

EATING TOGETHER

GOING FURTHER WITH THE HABIT

Gladness despite suffering

It is humbling and inspiring to be with those whose faithful following of Jesus through grievous suffering has resulted in a saintliness that we behold with awe. A striking characteristic of such people is their **Gladness**. The German pastor Dietrich Bonhoeffer is a well-known and inspirational figure. Less well-known, but just as inspirational, is a lady called Joy from Stourbridge whose story is shared in Andrew Roberts' book *Holy Habits* (Malcolm Down Publishing, 2016).

> Joy was orphaned as a young child. After basic schooling, she began work in a laundry before going on to various cleaning jobs. She never married and lived in a small council bungalow with her cat. In worldly terms, she achieved very little. In kingdom terms, she achieved more than most of us.
>
> Like Paul many years before, she learnt the art of contentment (Philippians 4:11). One day I visited her in her home and found her with two friends contentedly listening to the radio and enjoying a big pot of tea. If I had given them a million pounds, they could not have been happier.
>
> Joy was faithful in prayer, reading the Bible (gratefully accepting help as her reading was not strong), worship and fellowship and, like the widow commended by Jesus (Mark 12:41–44), she gave generously of her time and financial resources. Her purse was always open when there was a charitable event or a disaster appeal. And her cleaning skills kept the chapel spotless.
>
> Joy taught me so much. I had never been very comfortable with the Good News Bible's use of the word 'happy' rather than 'blessed' in the beatitudes of Jesus – until the day Joy showed me the happiness of being blessed even when suffering. As she lay in her hospice bed, she looked at me and said, 'Andrew, I'm so happy.' Almost invisible due to cancer but translucent with joy, this saintly lady was so happy to have enjoyed her life; she was happy for the care and love of friends old and new; and so happy at the prospect of being with Jesus. The happiest person I have ever met.

You might like to spend some time with the Good News translation of the beatitudes (either Matthew 5:3–13 or Luke 6:20–23) and reflect on how these attitudes, or ways of being, can be lived with **Gladness and Generosity**.

Creative movement and dance

One Sunday morning, the children came in for their blessing and, having knelt at the rail, two little girls, holding hands, skipped back to their seats with big smiles on their faces. This resulted in some smiles from the congregation and also some disapproving looks, as you might expect. Surely these two little girls were just expressing their **Gladness**?

Psalm 150:4 encourages us to praise God with dance and Psalm 30:11 talks of joy and thanksgiving being expressed in dance. In a church in the Northern Province of Rwanda, an area particularly badly affected by the genocide, the congregation started to dance with **Gladness**, taking visitors' hands to encourage them to dance. Their mourning was being turned into dancing (Psalm 30:11).

How often have you found yourself tapping your feet to some music or having a skip in your step when something good has happened? But how often have you danced with joy in worship in church? It has not been part of our culture in the way it is in parts of Africa and, although we might enjoy watching children skip and dance, we don't often encourage that in church – and yet it is the most natural thing to do.

Many people enjoy barn dances. The Iona song 'Dance and sing, all the earth' is written to a traditional Scottish tune (Pulling Bracken) and is ideal for a dance in sets of six or eight or a circle dance. You can use one you learned at a barn dance and use it to celebrate creation. Dances done together with others can also be used to celebrate community.

In the same way that musicians use their gifts to praise God and to encourage others to praise God, so can dancers. Different styles are appropriate for different occasions, so whether you have learned traditional Indian dance, ballroom or classical ballet, they can all be used in worship.

Various props may also be used in dance – flags, ribbons, scarves and larger lengths of fabric. Consider why you might use one of these, what colour it should be to fit in with your theme and whether you have the space to use it safely.

Many styles of music can be used for dance – it is your personal preference – but here are some suggestions.

For slower tempo, free dance: 'Lord, I come to you', 'Overwhelmed by love', 'My Jesus, my Saviour'.

For faster tempo group dance: 'When the Spirit of the Lord', 'You shall go out with joy', 'Teach me to dance to the beat of your heart'.

Some hymns are also suitable, for example 'Great is thy faithfulness'.

Dance is always easier taught in a practical session – a class or workshop – than from a book. There are many such sessions available and also teachers who may be invited to lead a workshop specifically for your fellowship. Contact the Christian Dance Fellowship of Britain (**www.cdfb.org.uk**) or the International Christian Dance Fellowship (**www.icdf.com**) for further information.

Sharing your story

If you know it, tell people the fictional story of Pollyanna (more information about the film version on p. 55), a girl who encouraged people to find things to be glad about, whatever their circumstances. Some of the quotes below might help (from Eleanor H. Porter, *Pollyanna*).

> What men and women need is encouragement. Their natural resisting powers should be strengthened, not weakened… Instead of always harping on a man's faults, tell him of his virtues. Try to pull him out of his rut… Hold up to him his better self, his real self that can dare and do and win out!… People radiate what is in their minds and in their hearts…

> 'Oh, yes,' nodded Pollyanna, emphatically. 'He [her father] said he felt better right away, that first day he thought to count [his blessings]. He said if God took the trouble to tell us 800 times [in the Bible] to be glad and rejoice, he must want us to do it.'

Each week, as part of your prayers of thanksgiving in church or in your small group, invite people to share things which they are glad about, and write some of them up as a testimony to what God is doing in their lives.

Could you write an article for your church newsletter or magazine (or local newspaper), challenging people to think about how they are generous with their time, money or possessions?

There are many films and books containing scenes about **Gladness and Generosity** which could be used as an illustration in worship. However, it is suggested that the following films and books are watched or read in their entirety and followed by a discussion to go deeper into the topic of **Gladness and Generosity**.

Films

👪 Alvin and the Chipmunks
(U, 2007, 1h32m)

A fun film for all the family about a group of singing chipmunks.

- What do the chipmunks' relationships with their record producer and the songwriter who 'adopts' them teach us about cultivating the habit of **Gladness and Generosity**?

The Blind Side (12A, 2009, 2h9m)

The story of Michael Oher, a homeless and traumatised boy who became an All-American football player with the help of a caring woman and her family, who welcomed him into their home and lives.

- What do you think motivated Leigh Ann to share her home and family with Michael? What did the family receive from Michael?

- Who might you welcome into your home – maybe not in the way Michael was welcomed, but for a meal or to be part of your home group or in some other way?

Dogville (15, 2003, 2h58m)

Dogville is a fable about what happens when a stranger arrives in a small tightknit community. At first, she is cautiously welcomed, but in the end abused and exploited by her neighbours. Her name is Grace, and the irony is not lost on us. She is, however, a much more powerful figure than the townspeople can imagine, which is their undoing.

Be aware that the film contains explicit images and violence.

- How does Grace express her humanity, and what can we learn from this fable about how **Generosity** makes us more human, more in God's image?

Elf (PG, 2003, 1h37m)

A hilarious Christmas movie for everyone. Buddy the elf, played by Will Ferrell, works at the North Pole for Santa. Upon discovering his true identity as a human, Buddy sets out for New York to meet his father, bringing **Gladness and Generosity** with him which isn't always as welcome as he'd want.

- How can we show **Generosity** to those who are very different to us, without being patronising or imposing our culture?

Marvellous (15, 2014, 1h30m)

A BAFTA-winning, feel-good film by the BBC, based on the life of Neil Baldwin, a man considered to have learning difficulties. Regardless of that fact, Baldwin sets off with an appetite for life, becoming kit-man of his favourite football team, a lay preacher, and getting on the Queen's Christmas card list.

- How does Neil's **Gladness and Generosity** speak to you and challenge you?

Pay it forward (12, 2000, 2h3m)

Trevor is given a school project to find a way of changing the world. He suggests doing three undeserved favours and asking the recipients to then do three undeserved favours to three other people, thus paying it forward. Based on a 1999 book of the same name by Catherine Ryan Hyde – a young readers' edition is also available.

- How does this film relate to Jesus' challenge in Luke 14:12–14?
- How can it help us cultivate the habit of **Gladness and Generosity**?

Pollyanna (U, 1960, 2h14m)

A young girl, Pollyanna (played by Hayley Mills in this classic movie), moves to live with her embittered aunt in the early 1900s. She introduces her aunt, and the rest of the town, to her 'glad game', and shows her determination to see the best in life. She soon turns around the attitude of the town, who in turn help her to see the good in life when tragedy happens. Based on a book of the same name by Eleanor H. Porter.

- Being described as 'Pollyanna-ish' is often a criticism of someone who is overly positive and doesn't live in the real world. In the film, what does Pollyanna bring that is wholesome and healing to others' lives? Is she unrealistic, or just hopeful about other people? How is she a gift to others?

Books: fiction

Are there people in your church or local community who would like to discuss some of these books at a book club? Guidance on how to form these is widely available online, and you could also ask denominational training officers for help.

The Celebration
Ivan Ângelo, translated by Thomas Colchie (Dalkey Archive Press, 1976)

When things or people change, we celebrate that happening, and the celebrations change our characters too.

- When did a celebration last change you? In what ways did it inspire or enable change?

†ŴŤ Danny the Champion of the World
Roald Dahl (Puffin Books, 1975)

Danny and his dad have quite an adventure poaching in the woods. The villagers work together to help Danny and his dad, showing **Generosity** of spirit but at the expense of the landowner.

- How does this challenge our understanding of right and wrong alongside a sense of justice?
- How could it help us as individuals and as a society to show **Generosity** to those in need?

†ŴŤ The Giant Jam Sandwich
John Vernon Lord, Janet Burroway (Red Fox, 2010)

Four million wasps have just descended on the town, and the pests are relentless! What can be done? Bap the Baker has a crazy idea that just might work, as long as everyone is willing to share their skills.

- What apparently crazy ideas have you seen to be effective?
- What crazy acts of **Generosity** might you be being called to?

The Gift
Cecelia Ahern (Harper, 2012)

A thought-provoking story of a man who comes to learn the importance of being generous with the gift of time.

- How do you show **Generosity** with your time?
- Do you exercise that **Generosity** with **Gladness**?

Humboldt's Gift
Saul Bellow (Penguin Classics, 2007, originally published by Viking Press, 1975)

Just what is Humboldt's gift? Just what is he giving? You'll discover at or after the end, but may not be able to put it into words. You will be entertained while getting there.

- How do you decide how you will use your gifts?

☺ **Waiting for Anya**
Michael Morpurgo (William Heinemann, 1990)

A book for older children telling of those who tried to help Jewish children escape Nazi Germany.

● How does this story challenge us to show **Generosity** with our time and even our lives?

Books: non-fiction

Five Practices of Fruitful Congregations
Robert Schnase (Abingdon Press, 2007)

Robert Schnase is Bishop of the Missouri Conference of The United Methodist Church. He discusses five practices – radical hospitality, passionate worship, intentional faith development, risk-taking mission and service and extravagant **Generosity**. Not all his work translates easily into the British context, but there is enough here to get you thinking further about extravagant **Generosity** and the other Holy Habits.

● What does the word extravagant add to the Holy Habit of **Generosity**, both theologically and practically?

Forgiveness: Breaking the chain of hate
Michael Henderson (Grosvenor Books, 2002)

A powerful exploration of the generous act of forgiveness.

● How might the power of forgiveness to break chains of hate inspire our praying and shape both our attitudes and behaviour?

Invictus: Nelson Mandela and the game that made a nation
John Carlin (Penguin Books, 2009)

The story of the amazing **Generosity** of Nelson Mandela in reaching out to the resentful and racist world of white South African rugby before the 1995 World Cup.

● How does the grace and **Generosity** demonstrated by Mandela put the issues you face into perspective?

👪 **A Kid's Guide to Giving**
Freddi Zeiter (Innovative Kids, 2006)

Written by a child for children, this American book is a guide to giving money, volunteering, donating goods and organising charity events.

● How might you encourage habits of generous giving at an early age?

Love Life, Live Advent: Make room for the manger
Paula Gooder, Peter Babington (Morehouse Publishing, 2015)

A little booklet with an idea to do every day. An Advent calendar of expectant fun and simple kindnesses.

- How might the principles in this booklet be lived in other seasons?

This Sunrise of Wonder: Letters for the journey
Michael Mayne (Darton, Longman & Todd, 2008, originally published by Fount, 1995)

A candid autobiography in which this Christian author shares all that has delighted him through his life and his sense of its eternal significance.

- What part does wonder play in your spirituality and discipleship?

Articles and online media

Unexpected generosity

A short clip from Soul Pancake on unexpected **Generosity** (youtu. be/2sPJSGDhpho, or search YouTube for 'unexpected generosity man on the street', 1m45s).

Give like God gives

A powerful clip featuring Bono of U2 speaking at the National Prayer Breakfast in Washington DC (**youtu. be/eOC5OApiT1I**, or search YouTube for 'Give like God gives Bono', 2m20s).

Reasons to be thankful

The fun-loving, cheeky Kid President gives us 25 things to be thankful for in this short video (**youtu.be/ yA5Qpt1JRE4**, or search YouTube for 'Kid President 25 reasons', 3m46s).

Charitable giving

The 'My personal giving' site from the Charities Aid Foundation contains reputable advice on giving generally, including gift aid, anonymous giving, charitable accounts and setting up trusts and legacies (**www.cafonline. org/my-personal-giving**).

The Theologian of Gladness

Thomas Traherne, a minister from 17th-century Hereford, mystic and philosopher, is known as the 'Theologian of Gladness' – find out more from the Traherne Association (**www.thomastraherneassociation. org**).

Imagining Abundance

This website was conceived by Julie M. Hulme, writer and Methodist minister, and reflects a lifetime of her personal and theological journeying in spirituality (**www. imaginingabundance.co.uk**).

A Generous Life

Resources for worship and meetings, courtesy of a special issue of *Roots* magazine in partnership with the Methodist Church (**www.methodist. org.uk/mission/a-generous-life**).

Good News Stories

Lillington Community Fun Day (**youtu. be/wcnD4dus2FE** or search YouTube for 'Good News Stories with Nick').

Baxter Job Club and Foodbank (**youtu.be/wF60wCMpHw4** or search YouTube for 'Good News Stories with Nick'). This story is also listed in **Serving** and **Sharing Resources**.

Music

The following musical items may help you to explore and reflect further on this habit.

The Penguin Café Orchestra and Simon Jeffes

A self-proclaimed 'blow against pomposity', some of Simon Jeffes' music is surprisingly familiar from adverts and TV programmes, in particular 'Music for a found harmonium', written for a harmonium salvaged from a pile of rubbish. Almost impossible to listen to without smiling and being glad.

Can you remember coming across an object unexpectedly which has made a positive difference in your life, whether in a small or large way?

If I Were a Rich Man, from *Fiddler on the Roof*
Jerry Bock and Sheldon Harnick, 1971

* Listen to the lyrics of the song to discover what Tevye would do if he were rich. How does that challenge our accumulation of wealth?

Amazing, Astounding, Extravagant Grace
Geraldine Latty, 2002

* Do the words of this song inspire you to practise **Gladness and Generosity**?

Can You Feel It?
The Jacksons, 1981

To celebrate **Gladness**, why not let your hair down and get dancing to some songs that make you feel glad, such as this or the ones that follow?

Happy
Pharrell Williams, 2013

An upbeat song that encourages others to join in celebrating the singer's happiness.

Reach
S Club 7, 2000

Another celebratory song that encourages people to harness the energy of **Gladness**.

Poetry

A number of poems are referenced below. Choose one to reflect on.

You may wish to consider some of the following questions:

- What does this poem say to you about **Gladness and Generosity**?
- Which images do you find helpful or unhelpful?
- How is your practice of **Gladness and Generosity** challenged by this poem?
- Could you write a poem to share with others the virtues of **Gladness and Generosity**?
- Making the Call
  Bob Cooper, from *The Ideal Overcoat* (Ward Wood, 2012)

The Messenger
Mary Oliver, from *Thirst* (Bloodaxe Books, 2007)

Unfurlings 10: Will You Build a Barn
Ian Adams, from *Unfurling* (Canterbury Press, 2015)

All Saints 3: Thanksgiving
Malcolm Guite, from *Sounding The Seasons* (Canterbury Press, 2012)

Mornings At Blackwater
Mary Oliver, from *Red Bird* (Bloodaxe Books, 2008)

The Elements of the Holy Communion

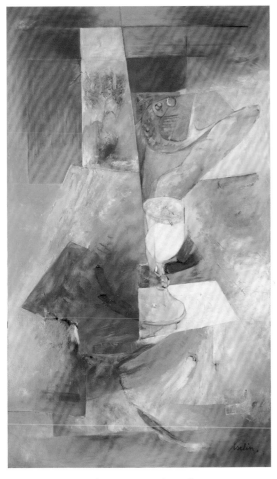

Jacques Iselin (1933–2003): oil, 1963, 180 x 105 cm.

From the Methodist Modern Art Collection, © TMCP, used with permission.

You can download this image from: www.methodist.org.uk/artcollection

Here we have a large, portrait-style canvas, somewhat reminiscent of a stained-glass window. It portrays the 'elements' of bread and wine, used in the ceremony of Holy Communion, but they are semi-abstract, sometimes suggested, sometimes amplified. The artist, a Frenchman, was active after World War II in a French association concerned with restoring churches in France. In this painting, and the three studies which prefigured it, he uses predominantly tones of red (associated with love and giving) and yellow (often described as the colour of generosity). Why do you think a fish has been added to the elements? You may find that John 21:1–17 helps aid your understanding.

- How do the symbols, shapes and fragments in the painting speak to you?
- How does this image speak to you of **Gladness and Generosity**?
- Draw or paint something that represents **Gladness and Generosity** to you.

Smiles and hugs

This picture, from a project working with refugees and asylum seekers, demonstrates **Gladness and Generosity** in the delivery of the project, which is picked up and passed on. All have the opportunity to be both givers and receivers.

- What activities are you or your church engaged in that enable the givers to receive, and the receivers to give?
- How might that underlying attitude affect everything that you do?

Credits

In addition to the Holy Habits editorial/development team, contributions to this booklet also came from: Gail Adcock, Gill Barber, John Barnett, Danny Brierley, Tina Brooker, Alex Dunstan, John Ellis, Rachel Frank, Dorothy Graham, Caroline Homan, Ian Howarth, Ken Howcroft, Helen Jobling, Sarah Middleton, Tom Milton, Lawrence Moore, Salome Noah, Kathryn Price, Marjorie Roper, Annette Sampson, Jan Scott, Sue Walker and Karen Webber.

'This set of ten resources will enable churches and individuals to begin to establish "habits of faithfulness". In the United Reformed Church, we are calling this process of developing discipleship, "Walking the Way: Living the life of Jesus today" and I have no doubt that this comprehensive set of resources will enable us to do just that.'
Revd Richard Church, Deputy General Secretary (Discipleship), United Reformed Church

'Here are some varied and rich resources to help further deepen our discipleship of Christ, encouraging and enabling us to adopt the life-transforming habits that make for following Jesus.'
Revd Dr Martyn Atkins, Team Leader & Superintendent Minister, Methodist Central Hall, Westminster

'The Holy Habits resources will help you, your church, your fellowship group, to engage in a journey of discovery about what it really means to be a disciple today. I know you will be encouraged, challenged and inspired as you read and work your way through each chapter. There is lots to study together and pray about, and that can only be good as our churches today seek to bring about the kingdom of God.'
Revd Loraine Mellor, President of the Methodist Conference 2017/18

'The Holy Habits resources help weave the spiritual through everyday life. They're a great tool that just get better with use. They help us grow in our desire to follow Jesus as their concern is formation not simply information.'
Olive Fleming Drane and John Drane

'The Holy Habits resources are an insightful and comprehensive manual for living in the way of Jesus in the 21st century: an imaginative, faithful and practical gift for the church that will sustain and invigorate our life and mission in a demanding world. The Holy Habits resources are potentially transformational for a church.'
Revd Ian Adams, Mission Spirituality Adviser for Church Mission Society

'To understand the disciplines of the Christian life without practising them habitually is like owning a fine collection of soap but never having a wash. The team behind Holy Habits knows this, which is why they have produced these excellent and practical resources. Use them, and by God's grace you will grow in holiness.'
Paul Bayes, Bishop of Liverpool

'The Holy Habits resources are a rich mine of activities for all ages to help change minds, attitudes and behaviours. I love the way many different people groups are represented and celebrated, and the constant references to the complex realities of 21st-century life.'
Lucy Moore, Founder of BRF's Messy Church